Bootstraps Laced With Faith

Resilience Through Life's Hardships

To my friend Ray,
Thank you for all
you do in the lives
of foster kids
Love, [signature] Eph. 3:20

Bootstraps Laced With Faith

Resilience Through Life's Hardships

Dinae Knox

Founder of Pro Se Services, NFP.

TATE PUBLISHING
AND ENTERPRISES, LLC

This book is designed to provide accurate and authoritative information with regard to the subject matter covered. This information is given with the understanding that neither the author nor Tate Publishing, LLC is engaged in rendering legal, professional advice. Since the details of your situation are fact dependent, you should additionally seek the services of a competent professional.

Published by Tate Publishing & Enterprises, LLC
127 E. Trade Center Terrace | Mustang, Oklahoma 73064 USA
1.888.361.9473 | www.tatepublishing.com

Tate Publishing is committed to excellence in the publishing industry. The company reflects the philosophy established by the founders, based on Psalm 68:11,
"The Lord gave the word and great was the company of those who published it."

Published in the United States of America

ISBN: 978-1-62854-231-8
1. Biography & Autobiography / Personal Memoirs / Christianity
2. Self-Help / Abuse
14.01.27

This book is dedicated to every child who have likewise had traumatic experiences. May you be encouraged by my testimony and empowered to chart your own journey towards a resilient recovery.

Acknowledgements

To God: You are *truly* the ONLY reason why I live, and move, and have my being. Thank you for the testimony You have given to me and Your unfailing love, grace, and mercy.

To my best friend and husband…Tony: Thank you for loving me the way I was and for who I am. I love you to Eternal Life.

To the loves of my life…Iliyah and Imani: May you always carry Jesus Christ in your hearts. I love you both so very, very much.

To Tate Publishing: Thank you for accepting my story and believing in my vision. Joseph Emnace, Gram Telen, and Dindo Contento, you guys ROCK!

To every person that I have wronged on my journey to recovery: I'm sorry; please forgive me."

Table of Contents

Introduction

It is good for me that I have been afflicted; that I might learn thy statutes.

Psalms 119:71 (KJV)

Many of the details of my fourteen years—April 1984 to November 1998—of experience in foster care and growing up as an underserved child are omitted or not elaborated upon because the purpose of this work is not to solicit a response of pity or to serve as an indictment of any social welfare system, but for me to sacrificially become transparent. My goal is to show how my faith in God has given me a resilient recovery; and to deliver a testimony of hope to vulnerable and heartbroken individuals, who are burdened by or has suffered from childhood trauma by expressing that we—foster kids, troubled youth, children of alcoholics, children of drug addicts, children of pedophiles, children from single-parent homes, children of gang members or from gang-dominant communities, children of teenagers, children of felons, or any child/youth that is a product of hardship—have the ability to become persons of excellence despite our past.

I do not mean a person of excellence by the measurement of material possessions or by obtaining high social status but by securing a stable foundation and sound mind. It is my belief that a person's wealth is not measured by their stature, but by their mental, physical, and spiritual well-being. That's not to say that one shouldn't strive for material possessions or social status—one should definitcly strive for greatness—yet it is my belief that one should not allow things that may pass with them into death to consume or define their personality. That's to say that a person of excellence is one that possesses an admirable attitude and character and strives to deliver their best performance in all their responsibilities and tasks.

In my experience and on my journey toward healing and success, I have found that a stable foundation in God is a great start to not only securing a sound mind, but favor with God and man. What I mean is: when one has been an abused and neglected foster child from the age of two to seventeen; when one has only known hardship; when one has had no positive influences to motivate them; when one has fulfilled all of the negative, statistical predictions against their destiny; when the odds are always stacked up against them; and when, somehow, a testimony of triumphant recovery with purpose is obtained, then one should believe that there is hope for the delinquent, orphaned, neglected, and underserved child. And, I believe such hope is found with faith in God.

At moments, some of the material presented in this book may be hard to read—my journey has taught me that no matter how difficult truth telling and transparency may be, they are required for a resilient recovery and a prosperous future. I present some of my experiences as raw and revealing as possible so that you can get a deep sense of what it is like for a person to suffer, survive, and triumph a childhood of trauma.

As a supplement to this book, I have created a self-help journal for individuals who have likewise had traumatic experiences and are willing to confront the ANTs (Abuse, Neglect, and Trauma) in their childhood. The activities and questions in the self-help journal are designed to encourage these individuals to accept their childhood and losses, so that they are no longer "excuses" for their failures and lack of achievements, opportunities, and resources. Whether you have suffered excessive corporeal, emotional or sexual abuse, severe abandonment, or any type of hardship, you can chart a path toward a resilient recovery.

In digging for the truth in my case files and writing this book, I found myself having to relive horrific events from my childhood in order to discover the source of my distrustful and hostile attitude and behaviors—a difficult task, but one well worth the effort. While on the road to recovery, I was able to initiate the process of healing the hurting little girl within me, victoriously overcome many of the adverse effects from the traumas I suffered throughout my childhood, get married, end the cycle of abuse and victimization in raising my two daughters, and improve my future.

I hope that my story will not only inspire recovery in

children and youth of hardship or trauma, but will also inspire people of stature to lend a helping hand, listening ear, or soft shoulder to these children on their journey. Besides, in my opinion, ratings, reputations, and research/ statistics only prove that those who have the ability and power to improve the lives of those in need, have not done so effectively.

I am very grateful to everyone who has contributed to my success, showed me tough love, and challenged me to succeed in life by my own bootstraps laced with faith.

Why Me...Because...

*When my father and my mother forsake me, then the
Lord will take me up.*

Psalms 27:10 (KJV)

Why was I Abused?

"I don't know! Mommy was hitting me with her whip; she
dropped me on the floor; and, when I tried to get up, I
couldn't. Mommy noticed that I couldn't move my right
arm and she panicked, then grabbed me by my waist and
brought me here to see a doctor. I don't remember how we
got here, but I haven't seen my mother since I was brought
into this room. Do you know where she went? Why are the
police here; am I in trouble?

"What's this? What's that over there? Why do I have
to wear this bracelet? Why do I have to change into that
gown? Ouch! It hurts when you touch my arm. My back
is too sore to lie down or sit back; can I just sit up? Why
do you have to listen to my heartbeat? It hurts to take a
deep breath; are you almost done? Why do you have to take
my temperature? I'm cold because it's freezing in this room.
Why do you have to measure how big I have grown? I don't
look like a big girl to you? Why do you have to put a tube in
my arm; what's an IV? What are those tools over there for?

What does 'surgery' mean? Why are they wearing masks? Are those computers going to stop beeping; it's noisy in here. I'm getting scared; I want my mommy! Mommy, where did you go?

"How many people have to touch and examine my body? Has anyone figured out why I can't move my arm or why I'm in so much pain? May I please have a bandage?"

According to the doctors at St. Luke Rush Presbyterian Hospital in Chicago, Illinois, and a report filed by the Illinois Department of Children and Family Services (IDCFS) dated April 2, 1984, I had sustained a "displaced transverse proximal of the right humerus—a clean break straight across." It was also noted in my case files that "such a break [in my arm] couldn't have resulted from falling off a sofa or was a typical break for a two year old…but was the result of pulling with force," and that there were "multiple fresh, finger-imprinted bruises on [my] forehead, left thigh, back, and arm."

After the doctors had fixed my arm, they released me into the custody of IDCFS. I was placed in my first foster home at the age of two until I was returned to my mother's care on May 30, 1985, after she had complied "with all [IDCFS] services in [their] service plan."

Why was I Neglected?

"I don't really understand the question!"

My case "was reopened when there was a report of

inadequate supervision when [my] birth mother was soliciting a sex act in the front seat of a car, while [I] was in the back seat…The police were contacted and IDCFS hotline was called…[I] was removed from the care of [my] birth mother on April 3, 1987, but returned to [my] mother's custody on April 6, 1987."

"I hate coming to work with mommy, it's creepy out here. There is nothing for me to do and no kids to play with. Usually, I sit here on the curb or stand against that wall and stare at the moon, when it's out, wondering how I could escape to it. Hmmm, does anybody live on the moon? I wonder what it's like up there. I wonder if it ever gets dark on the moon with the light always on."

"Mommy, can we please get on the bus or sleep on the train tonight, instead of going to your *daddy's* house? Mommy doesn't like me to talk to her when she's working, but there's no one else to talk to. Everyone always seems busy whistling at cars and getting in/out of them. Mommy tells me that 'she has to work hard to make enough money for her *daddy* so he won't get mad at her, and she doesn't want to make him mad because then he will beat [her] up along with all the other ladies who didn't work hard enough.' I hope my mommy earns enough money to buy me something to eat! It is ten o'clock at night and I haven't eaten all day, and my stomach is making a lot of weird noises."

"When mommy goes to work, she dresses funny and she changes her name. The boys usually call her, 'Hey Hoe,' and everybody else calls her 'Sasey.' Most of the time, she wears a short skirt with a tight shirt revealing some of her private parts; her high-heeled boots covers her knees; and she wears a wig. I'm not sure what kind of work she does out here, but it sure does keep her busy."

"I guess we are leaving now because mommy is getting into a man's car. She calls this man her *daddy* and tells me that he's my uncle. Hmmm, wouldn't he be my grandpa? What do I know; I never met my grandfather or this man? Why are they talking like that? Mommy, why are you sucking that man's private parts and what's that white stuff on your face? And mister, what are you doing to my mommy? Maybe I should close my eyes!"

"Oh my, somebody is in trouble again; the police just pulled up. Hello, Officer Friendly! Where are you taking my mommy? I guess we're sleeping at the slammer tonight; at least it's not the bus, train, or mommy's *daddy* house. Excuse me, Officer, may we please stop to get something to eat on the way to the police station because I am starving?"

Why was I Traumatized?

"Hmmm, what does *traumatized* mean, again?"

On November 16, 1987, "[my] birth mother was indicted for physical abuse after hitting [me] and causing [me] to have a puffed lip, cuts and bruises, and two black eyes… and [I] was found wandering in the rain in the aforementioned condition."

"Mommy and I had a fight but I knew better not to hit my mother back, so I just took the beating."

"Mommy, please don't…please stop…you're hurting me! Ouch, Mommy, please stop punching me in my eyes. My eyes are bleeding and the blood is stinging them. Wow, that hurts! What did I do? Mommy, I'm sorry! That cord hurts! It feels like lightning is striking my skin! I'm trying to be quiet; I'm trying to be still; ouch, that hurts, you're hurting me! Mommy please, I'm trying… please don't cut me…please don't burn me! Mommy, I'm trying to stop crying! Please put me down! Ouch, Mommy, I can't get up. Mommy, you hurt my head! Please stop; why are you so angry with me, Mommy?"

"Mommy had beaten me up pretty bad. After she threw me on the floor, she slammed my head against the wall several times, repeatedly stomped me in the mouth, and then threw me out on the streets. My head is busted, my lips are swollen and bleeding, and everything looks blurry. It's very cold out here and mommy forgot to give me my coat and shoes. I wonder where I would spend Thanksgiving, even though I don't have much to be thankful for; but, I sure would be grateful for something warm to eat. Right now, I am very thankful for the police, they always seem to come at the right time. I'm not sure what's going to happen to mommy or where I might spend the night, but at least for now I will be able to sit inside the police car and get warm."

By the age of six, my mother had been indicted for allegation number eleven for excessive corporeal punishment and my birth father was documented for molesting me. "[I] was removed from the care of [my] mother and placed with a maternal birth aunt until the age of sixteen... An extended birth relative who cared for [me] reported [to IDCFS] that [my] birth mother 'beat [me] for no apparent reason.'"

Again, why me...

"I don't know! Is there an answer to such a question?"

Perhaps the simplest justification for the life I have been dealt is that I was a child of hardship because my father was a drug addict, an alcoholic, a pedophile, a teenager, a minority who lived in poverty in a gang-dominated, drug-infested, underserved community. Or maybe the life that I was dealt should be credited to my mother, who, too, was a drug addict and alcoholic, a prostitute, a teenager, fatherless, a felon, a minority, and a single mother on welfare living in a gang-dominated, drug-infested, underserved community.

Or it could be that I was abused, neglected, and traumatized by my parents because I was the awful memory of their fornication; a mistake they were forced to deal with because they didn't have enough money for an abortion; or, because no one wanted to adopt a little brown baby that looked like me.

Hmmm...or perhaps I was their source for venting from the stresses of their lives: "abuse her to release my stress and frustration; neglect her so that I can feel needed; and traumatize her so that I can feel in control."

Sometimes, I wonder if my traumatic childhood somehow prepared me for a greater purpose in life. Perhaps, being abused equipped me with the emotional ability, gentleness, and understanding to minister to battered people. Could being neglected have helped me to understand the need for a charitable heart toward those who are vulnerable, heartbroken, heavy-laden, underserved, or at-risk? Or maybe the trauma that I have endured is what motivates me to encourage resiliency in others?

Perhaps, I was permitted to survive my childhood so that I can tell you the story of how I travelled on a journey for over fourteen years without any luggage.

Daddy's Little Sex Slave Paid for by Mommy

How weak is thine heart, saith the Lord GOD, seeing thou doest all these things, the work of an imperious whorish woman…They give gifts to all whores: but thou givest thy gifts to all thy lovers, and hirest them, that they may come unto thee on every side for thy whoredom.

Ezekiel 16:30, 33 (KJV)

By my seventh birthday, I had sustained a broken arm in three places (verified with medical and [IDCFS] documentation), four head traumas (scarring remains just under my locks of beautiful curls), multiple lip lacerations from being stomped in the face repeatedly by my mother (a permanent knot remains on my bottom lip), a fractured left knee which self-healed without any medical attention (yes, I still have the scar), and survived being beaten and molested daily by my father. Most of the bruises and scars that stained my skin, I removed with a skin bleaching cream because the memory of how the marks were sustained hindered parts of my recovery.

As a victim of my parents' adversities, I have had to sleep on doorsteps, at pimp-pads and whorehouses, on trains and buses, at drug houses, and have showered on the street underneath rain drops. I have had to survive on nothing but dirt grains, mud pies, and water puddles as nourishment. I have been placed in numerous foster homes, shared holding jail cells with my mother while she awaited same-day bail, and have been locked in closets for many hours while Mommy did what she did: drugs, alcohol, prostitution, slept, or entertained her guests. I guess you can say "I was a tough little cookie," but not by choice.

What about my father? You may be wondering if I know who he is? And I assure you that I do. All of my life I have known him as an alcoholic, happy-stick smoking, pedophile who disgusted me at the mere thought of his existence.

My father's disregard for my innocence and purity taught me to fear and despise men with a displaced anger. Any relationship with a male has been challenging for me to establish or maintain. I grew to have no respect for authority, position men often assume and abuse. The company of men, about ten years or older, made me feel uncomfortable. Compliments from unfamiliar men made me feel vulnerable to unwanted danger. Dating had its complication because I often wanted my "boyfriends" to play too many roles on my terms and conditions: like being the father-figure I desired to care for me, being the advice-giving uncle, and/or being the annoying brother who taught me the schemes boys used to take advantage of girls. Basically, I wanted them to be the "man" who wouldn't hurt me, but love me. My father never expressed that he loved me or treated me like his daughter;

but he did succeed in making me feel like the mistake he made with the woman that was supposed to only be a one-night-stand.

For over a year, my father abused and molested me at the knowledge of my mother. Every day, when Mommy left for work, he would welcome his self to my little body and private parts. Knowing that he was protected by my mother, daddy went the extra mile of having sex with me. In addition to manipulating my mother to provide for all his needs and desires, he bribed her for me. He would state promises "to live with us and not see his other baby-momma, if [mommy] gave him my body to toil with." It seemed like my mother was the pimp, my father was the regular customer, and my kindergarten body was the medium of exchange.

I remember a time when I was about eight years old, when daddy came over to my great-aunt's house to take me out. This was after I was taken from my mother's custody and I expressed to him how I didn't want to go with him because of what he did to me when I was younger and how I hated him. I remember him telling me that I needed to "move on, forgive, and stop living in the past." Huh, I wonder where does the nerve of people come from who hurt you and then try to determine the length of your healing process. As that day remains in my memory, I have this to say to him:

"Look, can you see the scars above my neck? Can you see the bruises below my collarbone, right above my belly button? How about the wounds below my pelvis, right above my knees? Daddy, these scars are from your venomous mouth when it poisoned my face while you ruffled my head and vagina with your coarse touches and slobbering kisses. These bruises are from your shark-like grip of my undeveloped breast when you would bite on my nipples. Can you see these wounds; these invisible and mental blood clots around my heart? Over the years, I have tried to avoid sharing with you the remembrance of this pain, but, Daddy, you had to tell me to 'move on, forgive, and stop living in the past when you never even said you were sorry. Here's a question that need to be answered, why the hell did you have to pollute my body, mind, and spirit with your problem of pedophilia?"

"Daddy, do you remember how you would whoop me, tie me down to the bed or a chair, and ruffle my body with your strength? I was terrified of you! Do you remember how I pissed and boo-booed on myself because I couldn't control my nerves? Only if you could have sensed how my blood trembled in my veins. Do you remember how I begged you to kill me; how I wished to drown in a sea of my own sweat and blood? Do you remember how I pleaded for you to stop penetrating against my vagina and screamed for help, and how you would cover my mouth with your hand? How about when I would try to run away from you and hide under the bed, in the closets, or in the bathroom? Do you remember how you would snatch me by my arm and ponytails and drag or slam me back on the bed? Huh, Daddy, the nerve of you to tell me to move on and forgive. Here's something you can hold on to: I wouldn't piss on you if you were on fire!"

"And, Mom, you scum from a dog's vomit, I regret the fact that you gave me life, though you have attempted to take it away from me since I have been born. Oh yes, I have questions for you too. Did you prostitute me out to Daddy while you were at work so he would be at home when you got there? You can't even look at me! You knew that he was molesting me every day, like a nine-to-five job, and would bathe me before you walked through the door because you hated to smell the filth of his abuse! Do you remember how on the weekends and holidays he would use my little body and force me to give his fingers a palm dance in front of an assumed ignorant audience? Oh, is that still a family secret? What was never a family secret is how you beat me whenever you felt like it without cause: rain, sleet, shine, or snow with whatever was in your reach, whether I was wet or dry, awake or asleep, standing, bent over, or sitting! Uncover your ears, Mommy, and come and rub your fingers across my wounds; you bet not touch me! For so many years, I wanted to tie an extension cord around your neck, hang you from a light pole and beat you naked with a bat in below freezing weather, while lightning burned you to death. Yes, I despise that you can still breathe in life."

"Daddy, why do you hang and shake your head low? Aw, you must pity me? Don't pity me, go screw yourself with a bottle of lighter fluid and then set it on fire."

"Here's a little pity for you, Daddy: do you remember when you licked my vagina with your venomous tongue and I crapped in your face? How about when you forced your penis into my five-year old vagina, and you watched me as I sweated and bled and passed out while calling for "help"? Do you recall every time I woke up from being molested by you, how you would soak me in a tub of burning hot water, knowing that I was already in excruciating pain? Did my tears excite you? Did my plea for death arouse you? Look at me, you perverted freak! Look at my tears! Look at my shame! Here, smell the stench and filth from your intoxicating saliva and venomous semen! Can you see the stained blood on my skin? Can you hear the raging voice of the little girl in me screaming in pain, 'save me'? I have tried so hard to cleanse myself from your filth, but no matter how hot the water temperature was, or how hard I tried scrubbing my body, or how much scented soap I used, or how deep the water was, I never was able to become free of your disgust."

Whew. This chapter may have been a little challenging to get through as it was hard to write. For many years, it was difficult for me to express the disgust, fear, and hurt from being molested because of the hatred I felt toward my parents. At moments, recovery seemed close to impossible but somehow, a few years ago, I was able to say, *"Daddy and Mommy, I forgive you for absolutely everything."* I credit such forgiveness and strength to a Force I came to know as God.

Transition One
From Mommy to Aunty

On November 16, 1987, I was found by the police wandering the dark streets of Chicago in the rain, battered, bleary, bulged, and blistered with a belly void of food. My mother threw me out of the house after she beat me up. By the time of this incident, mommy had been indicted by IDCFS on the eleventh allegation of abusing and neglecting me.

Finally, someone thought enough was enough! At the police station that evening, the process began for me to transition into a more permanent foster home.

I remember the evening being cold and wet, both emotionally and physically. I remember my great-aunt and her sister coming to the police station to claim me, as if I was a lost puppy. I remember their tears of pity for my appearance and physical condition. And, I remember hearing them cast lots for guardianship over me; I guess they were trying to figure out the benefits of becoming my guardian. The evening was long and I was tired of being asked questions about my mother and how I felt while I waited for all of the "legalities" to be processed so I could leave the police station with one of my great-aunts.

I was appreciative for my great-aunts coming to pick me at the police station, but I wasn't looking forward to the unexpected. I was happy to be safe from mommy and daddy, but then again I wasn't excited about not knowing if I was truly safe. And although, I was happy to be alive, I wasn't excited about my life.

I guess my great-aunt Maple won the coin toss because I ended up leaving with her on a journey that would yield ten more years of abuse and trauma. Daddy never showed up; he didn't show up at the police station or at any point in my life to be a father to me.

That evening was the first of three transitions that would occur throughout my childhood.

A Child for a Check

They that sow in tears shall reap in joy.

Psalms 126:5

After I left the police station with my great-aunt Maple that evening in November of 1987, I remained under her guardianship for over ten years. Ten years of more abuse covered up as discipline and about six more years of dreadful encounters with my mother and father. Though my aunty and her sons used abuse and trauma to discipline me, she never neglected to provide for my basic necessities: clothing, food, and shelter. Aunty provided stability, so that was good enough for IDCFS because they rarely monitored my case; I probably met with my case worker every other new moon before court, during school, or prior to dinner time at my aunt's house.

I grew up on the west side of Chicago in the Garfield Park area, went to Gladstone and Faraday elementary schools, and attended Carol Robert Center for Learning afterschool program. I attended Curie High School in Chicago and Larkin High School in Elgin, and then went on to college on a scholarship from IDCFS.

Although I grew up as an at-risk, troubled, and underserved foster kid living in a poverty-stricken and gang-infested community, I'm thankful for the opportunity to grow up.

Despite the excessive corporeal punishment—being beaten with broomsticks and extension cords for expressing the poor behaviors and displaced anger from the first six years of my life or for reasons unknown or untold to me at the time; even though I sustained a broken finger while being beaten on an infant stroller (documented by medical records); and even with having my face slammed into a radiator knob sustaining three broken teeth and not receiving immediate and proper medical attention (the two crowns and fixed chipped tooth still exist in my mouth). Despite the daily, slave-like treatment of cleaning my aunt's house to sickness; notwithstanding the daily, harsh emotional and verbal abuse of being called a "bitch," "never-gone-be-nothing whore," "trifling tramp," or "crazy"; and although being forced to lie about not being raped by a friend of my aunt's sons to protect them and having such incident plague my mind like an incurable cancer (documented by medical records, a police report and investigation, and IDCFS records). I'm still grateful for having grown up because if I haven't had the opportunity to grow up through my sufferings, I wouldn't have had the opportunity to become the person I am today even with my missteps.

I wasn't a perfect child. I had been riddled by abuse, neglect, and trauma. I can't imagine the challenge in trying to correct or raise me; however, I can't conceive that I needed such severe discipline either.

The adverse effects of being abused daily appeared throughout my childhood through my social behaviors and communications. My tongue was bitter and saucy, my disposition was "mad as hell," and my attitude was unpleasant to tolerate. Because I hated my life and existence, I wanted to let everyone know that I was miserably wronged and wanted them to either cater to me in pity or leave me the hell alone because I wanted somebody to pay for all the wrong inflicted on me. So, I am not saying that I wasn't in need of correction; I was definitely in need of correction from the errors of my ways and my negative attitude and behaviors that I was taught or exposed to. What I mean is that discipline used to excite control and fear, intimidation, and is unfit for the wrong doesn't correct a child.

Let me clarify! The occasional restriction for abusing a privilege, increase in chores for neglecting a responsibility, a timeout for disruptive behavior, or even a *loving* behind spanking is not, in my opinion, *abuse*. However, when chastisement comes in the form of being beaten out of the tub wet with an extension cord, having your arms and legs held while being beaten, being held in a chokehold while being lashed on, being whipped across the face, being beaten out of the bed with brooms, and being cursed at and having your character demeaned to crush your dreams; that is what I label as *abuse* because no love was expressed or received from those forms of *discipline*. In having my own children, I have learned that patiently training children to turn from their errors while lovingly correcting and guiding them is more profitable than trying to correct a child with abuse or trauma.

Family Life at My Aunt's

I never felt a part of my aunt's family because I was treated like a stepchild that came with a monthly stipend attached to her forehead to remind them of the benefit of letting me stay with them. My aunt was a single mother with three sons, all older than me. I called them my "home-cousins." Her oldest son was like the daddy because he had the authority to beat me; the younger son was like a brother because we were close in age and fought like crazy. My favorite home-cousin was her middle son because he was cool and I wanted to be like him. When I was in high school, I would steal his new or nicely starched name-brand clothes and wear them to school; yes, they were too big but who cared, I looked cool, at least I thought I did. My relationship with my home-cousins went bad after they forced me to lie about being raped to protect them and when I announced that I was writing this book about growing up in foster care, which included their home.

Despite the abuse and trauma that I endured in my aunt's custody, I was never homeless or hungry, and was always well dressed. My nice apparel was often pity-gifts from my aunt for "beating my ass too hard." I guess it was her way of *lovingly* covering the bruises and welts and helping me to conceal the real hurt and pain that I was experiencing and shedding.

Many people live and are fooled by deceptive outward appearances. I know, it was the case for me. Case workers, counselors/therapists, family members, the guardian ad litem, judges, and peers were all fooled by my outward appearances. They equated my decent clothing and neat hairstyles with a declarative statement about my well-being, overlooking the scars on my face, the cast on my arm, my withdrawn nature, and the explosive rage that wasn't the result of being well-groomed.

Have you ever wondered why some people that are experiencing pain don't appear to be outwardly suffering? Maybe it is because after being so beaten down by harsh conditions, those people have to appear strong or tough to avoid being a perpetual victim. I know that was the case for me. I pushed my hurt down but couldn't bury it; I walked away from my grief but couldn't run from its relentless pursuit; I medicated my illnesses with over-the-counter remedies that didn't relieve me; and I covered up my misery with cosmetics, washable materials, costume jewels, and gently-worn shoes. Every day, I rolled on a colorful glossy smile with blushed cheeks and highlighted, prominent eyes as an effort to mask the effects of the abuse and trauma that was tormenting my sanity. By this, I was somehow showing the world that I was *okay*, shaken but I have not been demolished.

Growing Up at My Aunt's

My childhood wasn't all abuse, neglect, and trauma. I did have some joyful times and learnt some valuable lessons.

For the most part, I enjoyed attending school and aftercare as well as celebrating Christmas with watching movies, playing games, and giving and getting gifts. School and aftercare were the places where I felt safe, had the most fun, and got in the most trouble. I am told by many that I was "something…bad as all get out, but smart as a whip… and was a fighter with a nasty attitude." Yes, I must admit, I was "something of an else." By no means was I tough, I was just defending myself; and being social was torturous because of the bullies who envied my *good* hair and clothes.

In grammar school, I was in some type of trouble everyday for fighting, being disruptive, or the know-it-all class clown. Also, I was a frequent visitor to detention and the principal's office. Fights with peers often escalated and became life-threatening because some involved gangs and I began bringing weapons to school. No, I wasn't in a gang, but I associated myself with people who were in gangs. As a result of my behavior and associations, I was expelled from eighth grade at the school I attended since first grade, and was on the verge of expulsion at the new school that I was transferred to within only a few months. I was troubled, but "smart as a whip." The only thing that kept me off the honor roll was my conduct, every other subject I aced. I was placed in gifted classes and had invitations to study at colleges, and even tutored kids older than myself. But my conduct—proper behavior—hindered me greatly because I was emotionally wired on rage.

Thinking things would get better, my aunty transferred me to a school closer to her home but little did we know things would only get worse. In only a few months, prior to graduating from eighth grade at the new school, I had been arrested twice for fighting and carrying butcher knives to school. I was almost jumped on by a group of girls, in eight grade and high school, which were in a gang called Traveling Vice Lords because they said "I was stuck-up and thought my hair was pretty." I was ready to fight—though I was likely going to get beat up, who cared? I was defending myself. The altercation between those girls and I never escalated to a fight because a security guard from the grammar school intervened and snatched me by the waist, right before the gang leader was about to shank me with a knife. Whew...I guess I was saved by the bell.

Jealousy and covetousness among females over hair, appearance, and fashion can really be detrimental in developing healthy relationships with peers—I know it was for me. Little to the knowledge of those that coveted my outward appearance, I hated almost everything about myself. In my mind, I was far from "stuck-up;" I was just withdrawn because I didn't trust anybody. I acted like a know-it-all only because I wanted to show somebody that I knew something. But, I guess I had a poor way of communicating the aforementioned thoughts because receiving acts of kindness from peers wasn't common or authentic.

High school wasn't much different from grammar school. I was still disruptive in class, trying to teach the teacher, still trying to be popular by being a class clown, and still fighting. My clothing that fit weren't always brand-named but decent, my shoes were nice but not popular, and I had a coat/jacket to match almost every outfit regardless of the weather. My everyday hairstyle included a bang that covered one side of my face and part of my neck, pasted in place with hair gel.

My eyes always looked closed because though I desperately needed glasses, my aunty never bought me ones that fit properly or were the right corrective prescription, so I saw life through harshly squinted eyes. My hygiene stayed intact because it was not an option to live in my aunt's house with a foul stench coming from your body. If I had a body odor of any kind, I was ridiculed, scolded, or beaten and treated like an animal. Hygiene was more important than health in my aunt's house. This was evident by my thirteen cavities, poor vision, and overall poor health when my health was evaluated at the age of sixteen under new guardianship. Hmmm…nobody really cared if I felt well as long as I appeared to be doing fine. I believe the only valuable lesson that I have learned while under my aunt's guardianship was the importance of maintaining my hygiene.

Because of my move to Elgin by IDCFS, I attended two high schools. I wasn't very popular in high school with anybody. I didn't fit into any of the popular cliques, clubs, or groups. Boys weren't interested because I wasn't sexually active and girls weren't very friendly because I was materially too much competition. I didn't fight as much in high school as I did in grammar school, but I did have a mouth that would kindle a fire that I always couldn't put out.

At Curie High School in Chicago, I had two friends, Sharee and Tia. Sharee and I grew apart after she became pregnant with her first child. Tia and I became enemies after I lost a fight for her, which became one of the most memorable events of my sophomore year. It was a fight with a girl named GiGi. I probably should've let Tia fight her own battle because I lost that fight in flying colors in front of what seemed like the whole school. High school became a little awkward after that fight, but I still had a mouth inviting GiGi to a rematch, saying that she caught me off guard.

I remember one teacher, Mr. Rancher, who I gave such a hard time that every time I walked into his class talking he would send me straight to detention. It seemed like if I wasn't in the nurse office for being sick from cleaning my aunt's home or too sore from a beating the night before, I was likely in detention. I was in detention so much that I would sometimes forget my regular class schedule. What my aunty didn't understand the more she tried to beat me to correction, the more trouble I would get into because I craved attention, desired somebody to hug me, wanted somebody to look past my tough exterior, and see the hurting little girl inside of me. I was carrying the throbbing pain from my father and mother inside with the wounds from my aunty and her sons on my back, headed down a road to self-destruction.

After I was moved by IDCFS to a new foster home at the age of sixteen, I was transferred into a new high school, Larkin High School, where my behavior changed. I only got into one fight, which was outside of school. While at Larkin, I joined the chess club and enjoyed tutoring peers in math. Peers weren't as concerned with my outward appearance as they were with my academic ability. There were still problems with girls and making friends, I believe for the most part because I felt different and it seemed like everyone knew that I was a foster kid. I will discuss the transition to Elgin in more detail in later chapters.

Childhood Interruptions at My Aunt's

The occasional supervised/unsupervised visits with my mother, brothers, and/or sisters; therapy sessions; visits with my case workers; and court appearances, in my opinion, were all "interruptions" because I have not been able to identify any positive effects they have had on my life.

My mother never appeared to be working to get custody back over me, so I didn't understand why I had to attend her progress hearings, court dates, or endure her poor efforts of trying to be kind to me. I was told by my aunt that my mother's parental rights regarding me was terminated when I was twelve years old and it was my fault because I went to court and lied that my mother beat me during an unsupervised visit. Hmmm…why would I lie? Living with my aunt wasn't much different from living with my mother. I didn't want to be with my aunt or my mother. I desired to be alone but that wasn't an option because I was under the age of 18. Besides, why lie to stay with my aunt? It's not like she offered to adopt me—I was only a paycheck to her.

My mother wasn't working very hard to get me back, so I couldn't understand how she had time to give birth to more children that I would grow up separately from. Visiting my brothers and sisters and, at a point in my life, living with some of them, only made me sick because I didn't know how to relate to them. I perceived their life as great because they had a childhood and a family that appeared to love them, lived in a big house, and was normal—they wasn't "bad."

Therapy was torturous! How was I supposed to express being upset for being abused, neglected, and traumatized? I was smart academically, but I was emotionally challenged. How are you supposed to tell someone that being abused, not having a mother or father, or a family with brothers and sisters all under the same roof makes you feel sad, guilty, and ashamed when you don't know the words to say at seven, eight, nine, ten…sixteen, or seventeen years old?

No counselor or therapist was ever able to explain to me the benefits of sharing my feelings with them. I still had the same problems I had when I left as I did before I came to the appointment. Huh, as experienced professionals, aren't they suppose to know that nobody wants to talk about hurt or what makes them feel sad, especially to a stranger? If I want to journal, I will when I feel like writing! When I want to express myself artistically, I will when I get the courage to! Besides, how does looking at black and white symmetric pictures help you diagnose my ability to reason or experience life? I wonder, because of the over usage of psychotic drugs in foster children, if medical professionals actually know how to help someone like me.? Hey guys, we don't need your tiny pills, we need seeds of faith; we don't need heavy syrups, we need the "well of water springing up to eternal life;" and we definitely don't need those tranquilizing needles pricking our skin, we need caresses of hope to soothe our minds, bodies, and souls.

Just thinking about the people or things that hurt me or made me feel sad only troubled me and made me want to express my anger in a violent way. Coloring, medicating, or painting a hurt out is not pain relief! Relief from pain doesn't occur until the victim accepts the reality of a loss of not getting something back or being compensated for something lost. It's like trying to breathe with only one lung that's badly damaged, or trying to ride a bicycle with only one leg, or trying to slice an apple with only one hand, or trying to love with a heart that has only two chambers clogged with bad blood. After having sustained broken bones, you realize that sometimes what's broken can be fixed—but my family or life wasn't broken, it was lost and couldn't be restored. It wasn't until I realized and accepted the fact that I wasn't going to have the family that I desired or be compensated for the trauma that I have survived when I became able to process the hurt, mourn my losses, and recover my life, which eventually I did on my own. It never made sense to me why I became solely responsible for restoring the little girl in me that I didn't damage.

Visits with my case workers were a waste of time and was always rushed. They always thought that everything was well because I looked fine. They never examined my well-being and when they expressed a concern, they was satisfied with the response of "I will get that done by your next visit" from my aunty. I learnt not to trust the case workers because anytime I shared with them that the "accidents" weren't accidents but abuse, they would go back and tell my aunt, who would only get mad and beat me for *telling* after the case worker left.

Court was a waste of time because nothing changed for me—my situation never got better. No matter how many times my mother messed up, she was always given another chance. No matter how many times I complained of being abused by my aunt, though I had bruises and welts, her explanations of the abuse being accidents always prevailed over my words. Besides, the judge never talked or listened to me, so why did I have to come to court. Hmmm…maybe the judge wanted to see how well groomed I appeared. It seemed like it was okay that my aunt abused me, as long as my clothes were clean, fitted, and my hair was combed.

Childhood Influence

In light of the calamity in my childhood, I managed to grasp hold of one positive influence—church. Church for me was a place of healing and peace. I knew little about the bible or God, but when the choir sang, it felt as if angels from heaven were holding me, caressing my hair, and wiping tears away from my eyes. The pastor of the church, Pastor Warren, was the first person to truly express to me the touch of love and teach me that God was my Father. Initially, I was confused by God being my Father given the life I have had. But after I accepted Jesus Christ as my personal Savior at the age of fifteen and was baptized, I understood how God was my Father through the spirit of adoption and in adopting a belief in his Son, Jesus. The following scripture became my foundation and hope in Christ: "When my father and my mother forsake me, then the Lord will take me up" Psalm 27:10 (KJV).

Going to church or believing in God didn't make everything instantly better. I was still broken, but having a foundation in Christ made the healing process tolerable. When anyone asks how I survived, I say, "I'm not trying to be religious but it was all possible through a force I came to know as God." Stunned, people have asked, "Are you sure it wasn't through therapy, with the help of any of your social workers, or the personal involvement of the guardian ad litem with your case because you were in the system for over fourteen years?" I smile and say, "No, just God." Because when I couldn't effectively express my feelings, when IDCFS wasn't there to intervene, when my father and mother forsook me, when my aunt and her sons treated me like crap and called me every name but my own, when trouble seemed to always sit on my shoulders, and while I was on a path to self-destruction, I must be honest, there was no other help but the force who carried me, called "King Jesus."

> *I [lifted] up mine eyes unto the hills, from whence cometh my help. My help cometh from the Lord, which made heaven and earth. He will not suffer [my] foot to be moved: He that keepeth [me] will not slumber.*

Psalms 121:1-3 (KJV)

My Cup Is Full

Yea, though I walk through the valley of the shadow of death, I will fear no evil: for thou art with me; thy rod and thy staff they comfort me. Thou preparest a table before me in the presence of mine enemies: thou anointest my head with oil; my cup runneth over.

Psalms 23:4-5

A few months after I was baptized, at the age of fifteen, the most dreadful, memorable, and scariest event of my life occurred. It was the event that prompted my loud cry for deliverance and help from a life infested with ANTs (abuse, neglect, and trauma), and it was the event that wounded me so deeply that its effects sometimes reappear through current relationships. Every time I visit my aunt or home-cousins, I remember them forcing me to lie about being raped. Every time my daughters are out of my sight or around boys/men, I worry about their safety. If my husband, or any man, becomes aggressive or rough in anyway, I become defensive immediately. This event made trust of authority figures, especially men, very challenging for me.

The event occurred about two weeks before my sixteenth birthday, on the night of Friday, August 8, 1997, when the journey toward home was diverted while receiving a ride home from a *family friend* of my middle home-cousin, who sent his friend for me after I called him for help to get home. The family friend decided he wanted to be compensated for his "good" deed. So, I guess he decided that I needed to pay for his services because he wasn't a taxi cab. No, the form of payment wasn't with money, but it was to fulfill his desire for my teenage body. The night became dark, long, and scary. The route included lightless city streets, cold alleys to confuse my direction, bumpy expressways that excited my nerves, and the destination was a gloomy and grassy park on Austin Avenue (near/in Chicago, Illinois).

Though my weak and hoarse voice echoed in the park for "help," and all my fleshly members fought, kicked, and punched, I lost the battle to protect my vagina. He raped me with his rough, flabby strength that wrestled my body to the ground while his harsh hand forced his penis into my vagina, ripping at my clitoris. Ugh… The ejaculation of his release made me vomit my breakfast from the previous week. After he was done violating my body, he further violated me by raving at getting "kiddy pussy." Once the physical trauma of his violation ended, he threw me in the front seat of his car, drove me home, and then threw me on the front porch of my aunt's apartment building.

After sitting there for a while feeling cold, empty, and in a complete state of shock, I wondered…why didn't my cousin come for me himself? Why didn't he call to check on me while I was en route? Why didn't he rescue me? Was I a favor for a favor? Why did he send him for me, when he knew about the nights that he would try to visit me in my bedroom at their home, when he visited him, while I was in bed?

Finally, I mustered up some strength to ring the doorbell.

"Who is it?" my oldest home-cousin called out from the balcony.

"Qua."

"Eww, you in trouble. Where have you been? Our momma is going to beat you!"

I was silent, unresponsive, and fearful. I was not in fear of the beating that I was expecting at the fist and whip of my aunt and her oldest son. I was fearful of being unprepared for the next attack, powerless over the next perpetrator, unprotected from more ANTs, vulnerable to and desired by older and bigger men, and leveraged for anyone's convenience. I became tired of being a victim.

Mentally, I was prepared to endure the physical and mental abuse that was bound to be inflicted upon me by my aunt or her son. I thought maybe the lashes from the extension cord would soothe my hurting and violated flesh and tear the filth of the rapist's touch from my skin, and as I screamed from being beat, I also would exhale the hurt and pain from being raped. The night grew more interesting because I didn't get a beating. I am not sure why or what prompted the absence of a beating, but I was spared. Perhaps it was the force that I discussed previously that was protecting me. Maybe God alerted my aunt that something was wrong through my appearance and unresponsive disposition, and maybe that is why my aunt just dismissed me to bed against her older son's desire to beat me.

Getting ready for bed didn't include my usual routine of eating dinner, bathing for the next day's activities, and brushing my teeth, but this particular night, I just went to my room, curled up in my bed, and cried all night long, wondering...could anyone hear my sniffles? Could anyone sense my hurt? Why didn't I get in trouble for coming home late? Did they know what happened to me?

This time, I did not look good, nor did I feel good. All alone with my taunting thoughts, raging emotions, and infested skin distracting me from sleeping and in the midst of my distress, I tried to soothe myself by reciting the following:

> *Shhh, little girl, my brain is aching with painful memories, my heartbeat is irregular because fear has consumed me, my tears and runny nose have bathed my upper body with a cold damp moisture. Shhh, little girl, I desire for you to hurt no more but I can't get my heart to stop pumping oxygen to my organs or my blood to stop flowing through my veins. Shhh, little girl, it's becoming too challenging to hide you because those that abuse you, neglect you, and traumatize you are too powerful for me to withstand, and I can't protect your innocence any longer. Shhh, little girl, I no longer can bear you—my arms and legs are weak, my strength has failed me, my hands are useless, and my bones are feeble because "love"*

has damaged me. Shhh, little girl, I can sense your pain but I'm no longer optimistic of gentleness, my touch too has grown rough and defensive and my speech cold and crucifying. Please, shhh, little girl, I no longer can listen to your moans and groans, the stench from this present wound has nauseated me to emotional deafness. Little girl, I can no longer answer your questions of whom, what, when, and why, but somehow, little girl, a stronger force will have to comfort thee now.

Saturday was a silent day. While doing my chores, I tried to be as invisible as possible. Throughout the day, I often drifted into fairytale-like daydreams to tranquilize my thoughts, my desires, my emotions, and my aspirations to live or engage in life, trying to escape and suppress the shock from the night before.

Sunday was eventful, and I was still without a shower. The filth of rape that had now been on my body for two days felt branded to my skin. I knew nothing about sexually transmitted diseases of any type, but if he had one, I surely now had it too. Even though I felt filthy, I just wasn't able to bring myself to bathe. Besides, water and soap never made me feel clean no matter how hard I scrubbed or how long I soaked. I remember when my daddy used to bathe me after he molested my toddler body. I hated it because the bath felt as if the molestation continued as he would watch me soak in the tub, wash me with the washcloth, blow the bubbles in my face, and then try "massaging" my body with lotion. The simple act of bathing felt intrusive because I still felt the threat of more abuse happening to my underage vagina. Merely taking off my clothes and bathing made me feel exposed and vulnerable to more imminent abuse.

On the Sunday after the Friday event as I sat in the third row of the middle pews captivated in the worship service. A spirit compelled me to release the burden of pain that I was carrying; as I sang the morning worship song, "What a Mighty God We Serve," with tears falling down my face, a spirit compelled me to reveal the secret of Friday night; as I clapped my hands, stomped my feet, and shouted an "amen," I suddenly became temporarily relieved of the shame of being raped. Fearing the unknown and exhausted from carrying such a heavy burden, I ran out of the church in the midst of the worship service, down the street to another great-aunt's home, my aunt Darcy, and told her everything that had happened to me on Friday night.

The next series of events was overwhelming but freeing. I was taken to the hospital. The hospital visit consisted of various types of invasive medical exams, a lot of blood work, and a lot of talking that I didn't feel like doing. The hospital room became primetime television with interviews from police officers and several medical professionals. Eventually, the home-cousin that the favor was for came and questioned me about the event. Initially, everyone in my aunt's home was sympathetic and everything was fine until their hearts became hardened as they received a threat from the callous-hearted rapist. I went from a child that had been raped to a "little, sneaky, lying whore." The rapist was a "big-time drug dealer" with many street connections and he threatened that if he had to go to jail for raping me, one or both of the older home-cousins was going to get injured for him having to be held accountable for his actions. Regardless of the doctor's report of forced entry, the rapist's DNA found on me, and the witness in the park, I was still the one to blame. In addition to that, I was forced to meet with the rapist under the supervision of my two older home-cousins that promised me that they would protect me, but they were really protecting him from the penitentiary and themselves from injury or death, as the rapist threatened. Because I was robbed of justice, I craved to execute revenge on everyone associated or disassociated with the rape. It felt as if an unknown "dark" spirit gathered in me. I became a very dark, devious, and vengeful person, not only at the rapist, but at the molester, the abusers, the neglectors, and the traumatizers. Simply put, I became a very troubled teenager and everything that I was at-risk of somehow found a way to affect me.

I later discovered that the law was trying to protect and deliver justice to me. A detective from the Chicago Police Department believed the truth from the doctor's reports and the witness in the park. But what the detective didn't know or investigate was my status as a ward of the state or my living situation. Being afraid of having her license suspended, my aunt lied to the doctors and police, saying I was her daughter. But had this information been known or investigated, he would have understood that my cooperation with the police meant unknown consequences for me at home. So I complied with the demands of my aunt and her sons and dropped the charges against the perpetrator.

Little to my knowledge, the detective did not give up and kept the investigation open. Five years, later at the age of twenty, came my opportunity to "cooperate" with justice and deliver peace to my own soul. I told the detective everything about Friday, August 8, 1997, including my status as a foster child and fear of cooperating because of the threats that I had received from my aunt and her sons. I cooperated with the detective enough to give him the information that he desired. After I told him everything, I didn't have a need to be involved with the investigation anymore, so I changed my mobile number, relocated to a different college, and began to finally heal from that Friday night. Honestly, I don't know what happened to the rapist, whether he was prosecuted or not. All I know is that it took me about seven years to bring peace to my mind and body after being raped.

Dear Detective,

Even though we never met a second time,
I thank you for being my angel of justice.

Mustard Seed–Like Faith

And Jesus said unto them, Because of your unbelief:
for verily I say unto you, if ye have faith as a grain of
mustard seed, ye shall say unto this mountain, remove
hence to yonder place; and it shall remove; and nothing
shall be impossible unto you.

Matthew 17:20 (KJV)

After the rape and sustaining more abuse, my strength to survive grew very frail as I was determined to end my miserable state. Some may say I was suicidal, but I say I was going to perform a mercy homicide because I was tired of being a punching bag, a piece of shattered glass, and an underage sex toy. I didn't need a shrink to give me a mental health diagnosis of being suicidal, depressed, or stressed. I believe anyone who has endured over a decade of traumatic experiences may be emotionally and mentally challenged.

I knew what was wrong with me and I didn't need a priest to perform an exorcism because they believed me to be demon-possessed nor a psychiatrist to prescribe me drug-filled capsules, tiny pills, or thick syrups to unnecessarily overmedicate my mind in an effort to suppress the hurting, painful, and revenge-seeking side effects of being mentally, sexually, and physically abused. My normal developmental processes was disrupted at the early age of two and continued with no noted end date, so no form of scheduled psychiatry, at the age of sixteen, was going to be the solution for balancing my brain, stabilizing my mood, or relieving my thoughts. I noticed from other people's experiences with psychiatric drugs that once the scheduled dose of medication began, the treatment wasn't likely to end and my problems were very likely to remain.

Yes, I probably resembled an individual with attention deficit disorder because I was anxious to end the life I lived infested with ANTs. At times, I probably appeared to be depressed because I had nothing to smile about, was smart but self-destructive, and consumed with fear of being vulnerable. On occasion, I probably resembled one that was bipolar because my mood depended on the weight of the burden that I carried for that particular day, hour, or minute. Sure, I probably was suicidal because I wanted to end my own existence in my world filled with pain, bring peace to the hurting little girl that was buried inside of me, and see those who have abused me be inflicted with a torturing death.

My journey to end my own misery came at a hefty price. After I complained to my case worker at the time about being abused by my aunt and her sons and that if she didn't move me immediately, I was going to jump off the balcony of my aunt's apartment building. I, further, explained to her that leaving me in her custody was like a death sentence, either they were going to beat me to death or work me to death. My case worker tried to ignite fear in me with her stern voice and threats to be placed in a mental institution where I would rot. I insisted that she take me with her when she left because knowing that I told the case worker the truth, my aunt and her oldest son was going to beat the crap out of me and work me like a slave. So she took me with her, not to another foster home but to a mental institution. Without evaluation from a doctor of any sort or approval from IDCFS, the case worker placed me in a mental institution with restrictions from using the phone and without a discharge plan.

Being in a mental institution did more help than harm to me—it was actually a blessing in disguise. The first thing I learned in the psychiatric facility was how to pray. I was confined like a serial killer without phone privileges: the windows were barred, the doors were padlocked, and everything was hard steel or concrete. I witnessed children and youth being restrained by oversized medical staff while receiving shots of some type of medicine with long needles in their arms, booties, or hips and afterward appeared to be in a zombie-like state. I have seen children and youth being drugged with capsules, tiny pills, and syrups that made them behave like villains or appear nervous or chilly all the time. Bottom line, if you were confined within the steel-barred walls of the psych hospital for a mental illness, suicidal ideation or verbiage, you probably already appeared or felt like death.

For the first time since being a baptized believer of Jesus Christ, I really prayed and put faith in that force that had often rescued me out of so many traumatic events. I once heard a pastor say "there are no atheists in a sinking boat." It felt like I was being hidden in confinement in an underground, mysterious hospital with an active graveyard without any privileges, protection, or rights. On the second night after the reality hit me that I was in a mental institution, with my bible underneath the pillow, alone with my silent tears and cold, I prayed:

> *Dear Lord, I don't know how to pray and struggle with meaning what I say. I lay here with my bible underneath this pillow because I'm trying to exercise my faith: maybe if I sleep in your word, you will deliver me from this place. Although I have no sacrifice to give, I trust the blood of Jesus be enough. I will spare your ears of speaking any vain promises because I am compromised with fear. I cannot commit to give you my heart because love is absent in me. I deny myself but am unable to take up your cross because no fight remains in me.*
>
> *Dear Lord, I am weary. Is this life what you have destined for me? Have I run my course completely because I need you to have mercy on me? I am scared of the unknown and there's no way I can flee. So, I lay here with my bible underneath this pillow with nothing but me.*

That night I slept in peace and the next morning it felt like I was free, even though I had no idea how I was going to get out of that place. Little to my knowledge, help was on the way! An employee at the mental institution had overlooked my chart and allowed me to make a phone call against the doctor's orders (I was on phone restrictions). But it was the mistake that I call "the grace of God." The phone call lasted only four minutes, which was long enough for me to call Lilly, the adoptive mother of two of my siblings and tell her where I was, when I got there, and who placed me there; and then the call was abruptly disconnected and I was forced back to my room. That phone call was one of the most important phone calls I have ever placed in my life and Lilly, and Sheila, my soon to be new case worker became agents of change, I believe appointed by God.

What seemed like a nightmare became a joyful daydream. The director of IDCFS was called out of a meeting and personally became involved in my immediate removal from the hospital and my aunt's guardianship, the assistant guardian ad litem came to visit and examine me at the mental hospital and recorded the physical evidence of abuse—someone finally listened. A joint complaint was filed by somebody against the contracted child welfare agency for confinement in a mental institution without assessment and my aunt. Lilly and her husband petitioned the court to grant them immediate guardianship over me. IDCFS placed the agency that managed my case and my aunt under investigation, and various other immediate and miraculous workings took place to remove me from my aunt's custody and the psych hospital. I don't have all the details nor do I need them; I am settled with knowing that prayer changes things through faith in God.

Finally, relief from a life infested with ANTs was only a few days away. Not only did God deliver me from that place but he delivered me from a life infested with ANTs, as well. Yes, despite being a troubled teenager having been in foster care since the age of two with a past of not only being traumatized but also now a delinquent; despite being too old for adoption and soon aging out of foster care; despite the group homes and shelters being full to capacity; despite all the odds against me, God freed me to a place I called home.

Only having known me for a few weeks and as parents of six small, adopted children, Lilly and her husband not only offered me a new beginning but a home free of maltreatment and the potential for a prosperous future. For the first time in my life, I was a part of a family with a father and a mother, brothers and sisters, aunts and uncles, and grandparents. Why would someone take in a troubled teen and later adopt them at the age of seventeen? I'm not sure but what I would say is that "prayer does work".

Transition Two
From Black to White

In February of 1998, after I was found and delivered from hiding at the mental institution, I was transitioned from my great-aunt's guardianship into the guardianship of the White's. My new case worker, Sheila, picked me up from the institution with all of my clothing from my aunt's home and drove me to the home of the Whites in Elgin, Illinois.

It was a day filled with excitement and happiness. It was like a going home and welcome home party but in an unfamiliar place. Everything was new except for me: new city, new community, new family, new home, new school, and new church. I even had a new name, parents, and birth certificate. I was transitioned from one life into another with the same body without any transformation in me.

> *They could change my name but not my nature; they could change my city but not my character; they could change my home but not my heart; they could change my surroundings but not my spirit; they could change the person who had guardianship over me but not my mind; so change into the new became difficult for me.*

Taken in part from a sermon
I heard by Mark A. Finley

Loving Deception

Thou, which hast shewed me great and sore troubles,
shalt quicken me again, and shalt bring me up again
from the depths of the earth. Thou shalt increase my
greatness, and comfort me on every side.

Psalms 71:20, 21 (KJV)

While I was being moved from one place to another, there was no development or healing taking place in me. I was given a new type of life but I didn't know how to live in it. It was like being transported to a foreign country without sufficient preparation.

The city I was from no longer was urban but suburban. The community I lived in was no longer predominantly black, dominated by gangs, or underserved but was a subdivision mostly populated by whites who seemed to have some level of success. The family I was a part of was no longer biological but adopted: my parents were no longer black but white; my guardian was no longer a single mother but a married couple; and my siblings were no longer cousins but racially-diverse brothers and sisters. The place I called home was no longer an apartment but a house: my bedroom was no longer a borrowed boy's room but my own beautifully decorated pink princess garden. The school I attended no longer had a large black population but was predominantly white: peers weren't so impressed by my outward appearance but my academic performance which helped me stay out of the principal's office and become more productive. The church I attended was no longer a family-like small congregation but an auditorium that housed different Christian denominational faiths. Everything was different, even the food, the way people spoke and smelled; I was totally unprepared for the culture shock that the new offered.

Just as unprepared I was for the culture shock, the family that took me in was equally, if not more, unprepared for the trouble I brought to their lives, home, and community. Prior to me, their oldest child was nine years old without a childhood similar to mine, and I was a sixteen year old damaged, delinquent, and despondent little girl in a teenage body.

Initially, I was excited about the new and the opportunities I perceived it offered. I felt that now was my opportunity to be a "kid," enjoy life, and grow up but then the rude reality of no longer being a child but a teenager approaching adulthood became apparent to me as I realized that time was irreversible. At moments, I was willing to set aside my anxieties, seek help to recover from the childhood I lost, and move forward. I was willing to unload the layers of hurt from my heart to make way for new love. I was willing to shed the scales of bruised and wounded skin and mend the brokenness in my spirit to develop new relationships. I was even willing to adjust and conform to the expectations of the new without complaint to show my appreciation. Essentially, I was willing to do anything it took to remain with the new family, and it appeared that the new family was willing to do anything to make me want to stay with them. It was like they were trying to bribe a bratty and ill baby with candy every time it cried, whined, or didn't get its way.

After about nine months of allowing me to have my way along with tolerating my disgraceful disposition, pacifying me, eventually became too much effort, energy, and money, so the fantasy-like life faded away and rules were implemented overnight. I was now going to be held accountable for my actions and choices, disciplined, and given consequences for my poor behaviors and language. I can recall thinking to myself:

> *Why now and not when I first came to live with you. Did you manipulate me with fairytales so that I would stay with you? If so, that wasn't necessary, besides I had no other place to go. Did you try to appease me until I was adopted, then teach me a lesson because IDCFS no longer protected me? If so, that wasn't necessary because you are the only people who have ever showed a real interest in parenting me.*
>
> *Yes, I took advantage of your kindness because you smothered me with pity. You were expressing to me that you were willing to compensate me for all the abuse, neglect, and trauma I suffered. Inevitably, we both learnt the hard way that trying to repay a debt that you didn't create to someone who has been severely shattered*

*for over a decade was close to impossible; besides, your
actions of trying to accommodate me with false love and
fairytales eventually made it hard for me to believe that
you ever loved me.*

Despite my chaotic behaviors of physically fighting with the White's, cursing and screaming at them, breaking their things and busting their walls, acting envious and furious toward the younger siblings, and embarrassing them in public, I eventually learnt to accept change and began to adjust, accept, and adapt to it.

I must admit that it was tough work but I persevered. In November of 1998, the White's adopted me at the age of seventeen and continually strove with me on my journey toward recovery. I managed to graduate from high school with a five-year scholarship from IDCFS. After living in the White's home for about a year and a half, I moved away to college and transitioned into adulthood at the age of eighteen. The relationship between my adoptive parents and I was never the same as it was when I first came into their home and continues to suffer to this day. So, I didn't receive much support from them while attending college or trying to mature into a productive and stable adult.

I was disappointed and hurt by their fantasy-like manipulations, controlling demeanor, and sudden tough love and began to believe all types of negative things about them. No, I don't blame them for our poor relationship (it takes time to heal and recover from trauma) or anything that went wrong while I lived in their home. In fact, in spite of our differences, I am eternally grateful for the sacrifice they made and unforeseen challenge they accepted in welcoming me into their family and home.

Transition Three
The Statistical Evidence

As [foster youth] prepare to leave care, they need support and services to help them begin the transition to adulthood and prepare for work and personal responsibilities. Studies of youth who leave foster care without a safe, permanent family reveal consistently negative life outcomes. One found that 25 percent of foster care alumni who aged out did not have a high school diploma or GED. Another study found that less than 2 percent finished college compared with 23 percent of youth in the general population. Over half of youth who aged out of foster care experienced one or more episodes of homelessness and nearly 30 percent were incarcerated at some point—many times the rate for other young adults. Youth who aged out of foster care were less likely to be employed or to have health insurance than were their peers who had not been in foster care. These negative experiences compromise these young adults' abilities to lead independent, fulfilling, and productive lives and create substantial costs for the government.

The Fostering Connections Resource Center. January 31, 2010. Number of Youth Aging out of Foster Care Continues to Rise; Increasing 64 percent since 1991. Retrieved from www.fosteringconnectins.org.

Nothing but Trouble

Therefore now amend your ways and your doings, and obey the voice of the Lord your God; and the Lord will repent him of the evil that he hath pronounced against you.

Jeremiah 26:13 (KJV)

The same week that I was going to be transitioning into adulthood on my eighteenth birthday in August of 1999 was the same week that I was preparing to leave for college. I had no support system when I started college or became an adult. My relationship with the White family had been severely damaged. I had no friends because of my ridiculously rude, defensive, and conceited attitude and it seemed that everyone had stopped trying to invest energy or time in helping me.

The only services that were available to me were those offered by the college, welfare, and my scholarship from IDCFS. Although I utilized the educational, financial, and housing services that were available, I failed to seek professional therapy to help me address the posttraumatic stress from my childhood.

After over a decade of not allowing myself to trust people, establish secure relationships, heal from past abuse and neglect, and learn coping skills to appropriately deal with childhood traumas, every choice or decision I made consistently produced negative life outcomes for me.

One evening while rejoicing over a wrong that I had committed to a person, my adoptive mother stated that "God was going to do something so intense to grasp my attention for all the wrong that I was committing to people…," and He did. Within only a few days, after I returned to college from winter break in 2001, I became involved in the judicial system. My poor behaviors and nasty attitude had landed me into a sea of trouble. I was on a road to becoming an uneducated criminal and emotional wreck. The research was correct; and I was now a statistic.

I was first arrested on January 10, 2001, in City One for lying to a bank and filing a false police report alleging that someone stole my bank card and made unauthorized charges. After I depleted the funds from my scholarship stipend, I had overcharged my bank card and overdrew my account to purchase school supplies and decorations for my dorm room. I served two days in jail. One hundred and seventy-six days of jail time was waived, I completed thirty months of probation, and paid over $2,500 in restitution and court fees/fines.

About a month later on February 12, I was arrested again in that same city for stealing money from my college roommate to purchase material items for myself. I served two days of jail time, 180 days of jail time was waived, completed thirty months of probation, underwent a mental/psychologist evaluation, and paid $490 in court fees/fines. The sentence of this offense ran concurrent with the previous offense.

After being expelled from one college with a criminal record, I transferred to another university in City Two and was arrested twice. I was arrested for writing an altered check on my own account to a college bookstore and telephone harassment in August and October of the same year. There was no jail time for the October arrest, but I spent Labor Day of 2001 in jail from Thursday to that Monday. If it not had been for the grace of God, overcrowding in the jail, and something called "a bond off the tier," I would have served over a year in county jail. I was found not guilty for both offenses.

Later that year, I tried to turn my life around; but with poor grades and a criminal record, it seemed impossible. It was hard to get a job or back into a four-year university. I was homeless and had no family support or friends. So, what did I do? Because I still was on probation for offenses committed in City One and had to report monthly, I moved back to that city. I found a room for rent, which I paid for out of my stipend, and enrolled in a community college. I survived off the remaining balance of my monthly stipend and refund checks from my student loans.

In October 2002, I got into an altercation with some roommates and was arrested for allegedly hitting one of my roommates with a car, leaving the scene of the accident, and stealing her CDs and sweater. I pleaded not guilty to the charges because I did not hit my roommate; she jumped on the car. There was no jail time issued; I completed twelve months of conditional probation and paid over $600 in court fees/fines.

Trouble seemed inescapable, and the amount of mercy that covered me seemed to never run out. I have truly seen Romans 5:20—"where sin abounded, grace did much more abound" (KJV)—in action. Taking advantage of mercy and the patience of the judges, a few times I failed to comply with my probation terms or court orders. Eventually, my probation officer got fed up and held me accountable for my actions. I wasn't arrested again, but I spent my first Mother's Day weekend in jail. As a nursing mother to a three-month-old baby, it was one of the most humiliating and humbling experiences of my life! In order for my daughter to eat, I had to pump milk into a bottle from a jail cell every four to six hours and have it delivered to my husband by a guard.

My involvement in the judicial system lasted for a about two years and although, by God's grace, I never served time in prison, I did have to dedicate about four years of my life to completing probation terms and repaying fees and fines, all while trying to obtain employment and stay in school.

The ability to overcome the judicial system with a repeat offender record, no college degree, no support system, and with a probation officer that I felt desired my head on her wall was very difficult. And to top it off, I still hadn't charted a course toward repentance or recovery.

I was a mess—on a path toward self-destruction and becoming an institutionalized criminal on welfare without a college education and wasted talents. My excuse and reason for it all was: I was a hurting little girl and a child of hardship for over fourteen years ravished by abuse, neglect, and trauma.

It wasn't until May 2005 that I *really* realized that my life needed to change—drastically.

I was already making amends for my actions by paying restitution to people, banks, colleges, and stores that I had stolen from or lied to and court fees/fines. I had about another year to go on probation, so I asked my probation officer to transfer my case to the new city I was living and building a family in, and she agreed. By June 2006, I successfully completed the remainder of my probation, fully made restitution and paid all court fees/fines, completed my paralegal degree, got married, and had my first child. I was making progress, but I was still hurting. So, daily I sought the Lord because I didn't know where to start and in frustration I often vented my rage to Him. In time, God saved me from myself.

Give me a moment! I have to process the truth because I have hidden it for so long. Whew, it's finally out! Oh, the sound of the shackles from all the wrong that I have spoken and committed while confessing the name of Jesus loosening from around my neck, my wrists, and my ankles.

Please, allow me another minute! Reality never felt so good! I have hid behind the shame of my childhood and being arrested and having a criminal background for so many years that it has robbed me of countless hours of peace.

I have allowed the strongholds of guilt of not completing my undergraduate degree by 2003 and becoming a lawyer by the age of thirty, wasting my scholarship from IDCFS and taking out student loans, not having a steady career, and being unprepared for children and marriage to send me into a state of depression while battling with bulimia, for several years.

Loneliness has been eating at my soul. Fear has been suffocating my heart. Embarrassment has been torturing my being. But today, I can finally say that I am forgiven and have sought forgiveness from everyone that I have wronged

Praise the Lord! My conscious didn't let me rest in sin forever!

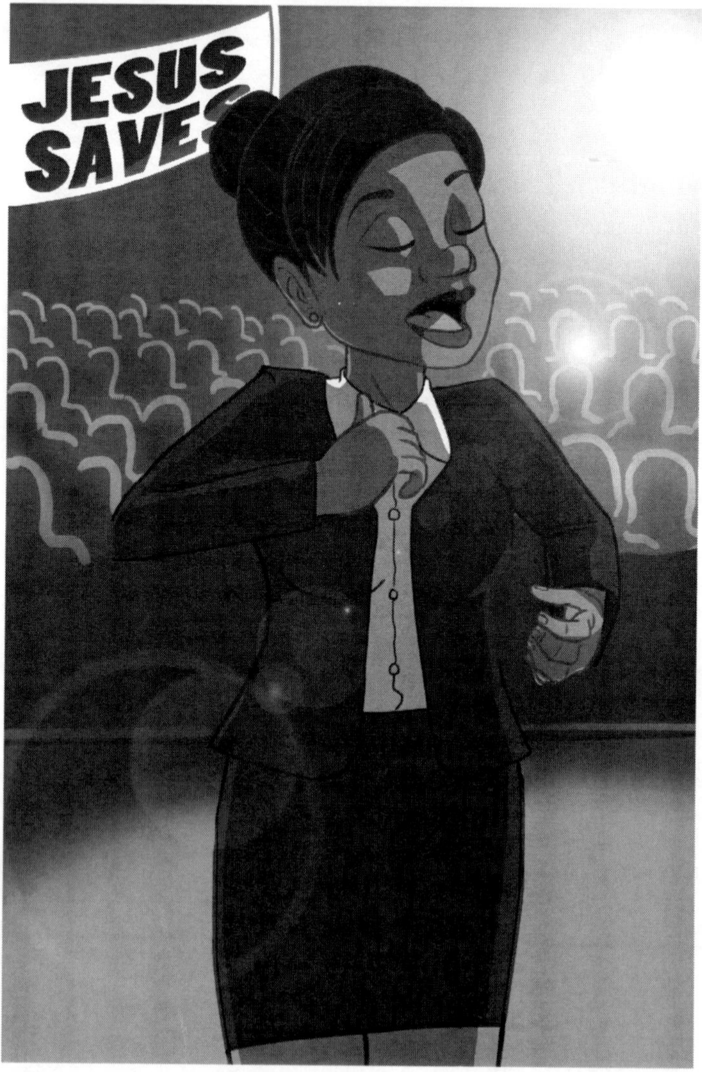
JESUS SAVES

Oh Yes, I've Got a Testimony!

But I will sing of thy power; yea, I will sing aloud of
thy mercy in the morning: for thou hast been my defense
and refuge in the day of my trouble. Unto thee, O my
strength, will I sing: for GOD is my defense, and the
GOD of my mercy.

Psalms 59:16, 17 (KJV)

Finally, at the age of twenty-five, I began my journey toward a resilient recovery. Not only was I determined to change the course of my life, but I became determined to rebel against the poor statistics regarding foster children and youth. The only source that I used was willpower, and a lot of prayer. This may be hard for some to believe but I must attest that the only reason why I still move and live and have life is by the generous grace of God. As stated by Corrie Ten Boom, "You may never know that Jesus is all you need, until Jesus is all you have." It is impossible to accredit my testimony to any person, institution, activity, or psychological assessment. Besides, every relationship I was a part of was either severely damaged or severed. And I was determined not to recover on the government's dime, so I didn't apply for welfare.

Secured with belief in the will of God for my life, determined to make amends and end all unrighteous acts, acting swiftly with eagerness while overcoming temptations to lie in defeat, holding on to my faith to reduce the doubts of success, surrounding myself in a sea of scriptures to combat the trickery of enemies, and with an attainable vision of a better life in my head, I went to battle for the hurting little girl within me until the stumbling blocks of inward hurt came tumbling down, and I began my journey toward recovery despite many missteps.

The first step I took toward charting my course toward recovery was allowing myself time to grieve my childhood. Second, I forgave myself and dismissed my pride and sought the forgiveness of others. And lastly, I kept fighting the battles of healing and making amend even when I didn't feel like it. Some of the hardest battles I had to fight were for forgiveness because hearts are not easily softened. When you break a glass, you can sweep it up, throw it in the garbage, and buy a new one, but when you break a person's heart the damage affects their soul, spirit, and body, so it becomes very challenging to restore a damaged relationship with mere apologies. I had to set aside my pride and *completely* step outside of my comfort zone.

I must admit that although I haven't fully arrived at my desired destination, I praise God for my progress thus far. As God is still chiseling my character to fully reflect the image of Christ, I thank God for the cutting and polishing he has done in my life so far to reveal my true beauty as a precious stone in the palm of his hand. As I praise God, at this stage in my life, I am reminded of when and where He has brought me from, carried me through, and is taking me to.

Despite my background, the Lord has blessed me to complete my paralegal and bachelor's of business administration degrees and study French and Spanish. Currently, I am in the process of completing my master's of business administration (projected completion date is August, 2014).

In 2007, I founded a not-for-profit organization, Pro Se Services, to provide hunger relief, nutrition and wellness, and human services to underserved populations.

I have written award-winning grants, published this illustrated, memoir and self-help journal, traveled the United States, and worked for several *Fortune 500* companies. Isn't God amazing?

When I think *Why me?* I am reminded of how God took a badly battered little girl and mended her back together and comforted and shielded her. Or how He lovingly disrupted a troubled youth's path toward self-destruction. Or how His hand gently caressed a distraught, ravished, and shattered young lady into a wholly redeemed woman.

When I read the statistics, reputations, and failures of troubled youth, children of alcoholics, children of drug addicts, children of pedophiles, children from single-parent homes, children of gangs or from gang-dominant communities, children of teenagers, children of felons, or any child/youth that is a product of hardship, I must proclaim the goodness of God by praising him that I am not where I could be.

And when I was able to embrace the truth about my childhood, missteps, and run-ins with law, I became resilient!

Charting Your Own Road toward a Resilient Recovery

The Companion Journal

This self-help journal section is comprised of seven exercises or strategies to inspire healing in you and to help you develop a road map for your journey toward a victorious recovery.

Section One
Why Me?

I returned, and saw under the sun, that the race is not to the swift, nor the battle to the strong, neither yet bread to the wise, nor yet riches to men of understanding, nor yet favour to men of skill; but time and chance happeneth to them all.

Ecclesiastes 9:11 (KJV)

The question of "why me," I believe, plagues the mind of any person who is curious or has ever experienced adversity. As I matured in my relationship with God, I learnt to ask the question, "God, if it has to be me, will you promise to carry me through?" Oftentimes, I still found myself broken, battered, bruised, and bent throughout the journey, but I must say into a person with a more temperate character and spirit.

Activity

Before answering the questions in this section, please take some time to define (from a dictionary and in your own words) the following words: abuse, hardship, neglect, and trauma.

	Dictionary Definition	Your Definition
Abuse		
Hardship		
Neglect		
Trauma		

Reflections to Journal

What set of conditions or events played a role in determining my childhood/past?

_____

_____

_____

_____

What situations brought hardship and trauma to my life?

_____

_____

_____

_____

Why were the abovementioned conditions, events, or situation unavoidable?

_____

_____

_____

_____

Who are you asking these questions of?

_____

_____

_____

_____

Section Two
Acceptance

When you can accept how you came to be who you are, where you are from, and what you have survived; then, you can understand why you exist and strive toward your destiny.

—Dinae Knox

In a world where outward appearances seem to be more important than inner well-being, it is important to accept and understand what makes us who we are.

Activity

Take a moment to reflect on your beliefs, community, country, family, features, habits, history, and interests.

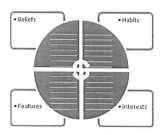
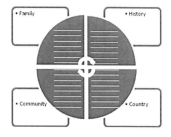

Reflections to Journal

Define the following words: accept, destiny, strive, and understand.

_____

_____

_____

_____

_____

_____

_____

_____

How did you come to be who you are?

_____

_____

_____

_____

Who are you?

_____

_____

_____

_____

Where are you from?

_____

_____

_____

_____

What have you survived so far?

_____

_____

_____

_____

Why do you believe you exist (What's your purpose in life)?

_____

_____

_____

_____

Section Three
Influences

Keep thy heart with all diligence; for out of it are the issues of life.

Proverbs 4:23 (KJV)

I believe the activities, ideas, people, places, and things that we have been directly or indirectly exposed to, accepted, became ashamed of, grieved, or found offensive are what we allow, more often than not, to shape our nature and our stature.

Activity

For the next seventy-two hours (three days), try to identify and list all, as many as you can, negative behaviors, thoughts, and words. Use the below chart to assist you.

	Negative Behaviors	Negatives Thoughts	Negative Words
24 hours			
48 hours			
72 hours			

Reflections to Journal

What caused you to exhibit the above negative behaviors, thoughts, and/or words?

_____

_____

_____

_____

Why do you believe you respond to certain situations negatively?

_____

_____

_____

_____

Identify the childhood experiences you believe contributes to the above negativities? Why?

_____

_____

_____

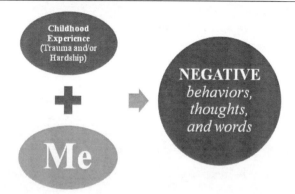

Section Four
Disruptions

Are you prepared for change?

—Dinae Knox

Frequent disruptions in one's education, home life, and social life may affect their ability to coexist friendly, develop normally, and secure stability. I have found that any change, for a child, without preparation, makes coping with change or transitions continually difficult.

Activity

Take a moment to remember a time from your childhood when you had to break away from someone or something that you were attached to, deal with an abrupt change in your life, or had to move from one condition, phase, or location to another without preparation.

Reflections to Journal

How did those disruptions or transitions affect you?

Disruption or Transition	Adverse Effect	Why?

How did you adjust after the disruption or transition occurred?

_____

_____

_____

_____

Section Five
Control

Sometimes we use fear irresponsibly to control the things we are afraid to confront.

—Dinae Knox

It is normal to try to protect ourselves from the things we fear, but it is not wise to try to control the inevitable things from happening in our life.

Activity

Define the following words: authority, control, fear, and protection.

_____

_____

_____

_____

Tonight, sit in the dark—make the room as dark as possible—for about ten minutes, then turn on the light and complete the below questions.

Were you afraid of the dark? If so, what made you uncomfortable about being in the dark? Was it a person or an experience that you had?

_____

_____

_____

_____

_____

_____

_____

Reflections to Journal

I have no authority to control _____, so I fear the unpredictable; how do I protect myself?

_____

_____

_____

_____

How do I prepare myself for the unknown?

_____

_____

_____

Why do I have to be in control?

_____

_____

_____

_____

What can I prevent from happening to me?

_____

_____

_____

_____

How much control do I have over those things which I cannot control?

_____

_____

_____

_____

Section Six
Forgiveness

I did not learn to forgive until I was in need of forgiveness.

—Dinae Knox

Forgiving The action of no longer feeling or showing anger or discomfort or having unfriendly feelings regarding an unjust or unworthy wrong, insult, or injury that you suffered

Being Forgiven The result of being pardoned from an unjust or unworthy wrong, insult, or injury that you caused another person to suffer

Activity & Reflections

Define the following words from a dictionary and what they mean to you: forgiveness, resentment, and amends.

_____

_____

_____

_____

List three people who have wronged, insulted, or injured you and how.

_____

_____

_____

List three people who you have wronged, insulted, or injured and how.

_____

_____

_____

_____

Forgiving and Being Mended	Being Forgiven and Making Amends
How has the wrong, insult, or injury listed in question #2 affected you or your life?	How did the wrong, insult, or injury listed in question #3 affected your relationship with the person(s) listed in question #3? Is the relationship important to you to restore? Why or why not? Are your reasons self-motivated or because you are truly remorseful for your actions?
Do you need an apology before you can forgive the persons listed in question #2? Why?	On a separate sheet of paper, write a letter to the persons listed in question #3 requesting their forgiveness. Also, use this letter to express how not having them actively apart of your life has affected you. Resolve to make peace in some way. **Try not to use the word "you" because sometimes it displaces the blame.** Keep the letter simple, don't beat around the bush.
Whether you are given an apology or not, on a separate sheet of paper write a letter forgiving the three people that hurt you in question #2.	Make an honest effort to meet the persons in question #3 face-to-face to apologize in-person. If a face-to-face apology is not possible, send the letter to them.
Now that you've gotten "it" out, let "it" go! Mail the letter to that person, burn it, or something, just don't bury it. Buried hurt always resurface in some form.	Move on!!! We can only be responsible for ourselves. Moving on means not being concerned with whether or not they outwardly forgive you, but whether if you have done everything in your power to inwardly make amends.
Were you able to let "it" go? Letting go means that you are no longer feeling or showing anger or discomfort or having unfriendly feelings regarding the wrong, insult, or injury that you suffered. If so, congratulations. If not, why not?	Making amends means no longer allowing the wrong, insult, or injury cause you discomfort, and prompts a change in attitude and behavior. If you put an end to inflicting hurt, then you put an end to seeking forgiveness.

The process of seeking forgiveness and making amends sometimes require more effort than forgiving and being mended because of our pride, selfishness, and ability to control our own actions.

Section Seven
Charting Your Course

Life is 10% what happens to you, and 90% how you respond to it.

—Unknown

The purpose of this section is to assist you with charting your path toward recovery to transform yourself into a person of excellence.

Why have you chosen to chart your course toward recovery? Explain.

_____

_____

_____

_____

Is this your first attempt at recovery?

_____

_____

_____

_____

What are your expectations of the recovery process? Why?

_____

_____

_____

_____

What would a person of excellence look like to you?

_____

_____

_____

_____

Do you have any role models?

_____

_____

_____

_____

How can you become a person of excellence?

_____

_____

_____

_____

My Roadmap

Where I come from and have been...

Hardships I have endured from 0 – 17 years old...	Traumas I have suffered from 0 – 17 years old...

Hardships I have endured from 18 – 24 years old...	Traumas I have suffered from 18 – 24 years old...

Hardships I have endured from 25 to present...	Traumas I have suffered from 25 to present...

Where I'm at…

Describe your current state in regards to the below situations.				
Education	**Employment**	**Housing**	**Health**	**Finances**

Describe your current state in regards to the below situations.			
Relationships	**Mentally**	**Spiritually**	**Emotionally**

Describe your current state in regards to the below situations.			
Criminal	**Government Assistance (food stamps, etc.)**	**Responsibilities (children, etc.)**	**Habits (drugs, alcohol, etc.)**

Where I'm going...

Health					
Finances					
Relationships					
Mentally					
Spiritually					
Emotionally					
Criminal					
Government Assistance					
Responsibilities					
Habits					

Describe how you plan to reach your goals with the...				
Situations	**Resources you currently have**	**Resources you currently need**	**Resources that might be available to you/help needed from others**	**What is hindering you from reaching goals?**
Education				
Employment				
Housing				
Health				
Finances				
Relationships				
Mentally				
Spiritually				
Emotionally				

Criminal				
Government Assistance				
Responsibilities				
Habits				

Epilogue

These things I have [written] unto you, that in [Christ] ye might have peace. In the world ye shall have tribulations: but be of good cheer; [Christ] have overcome the world.

John 16:33 (KJV)

Pro Se Services, NFP.

On April 4, 2007, Dinae Knox, a 14-year veteran of the Illinois foster care system, founded Pro Se Services, NFP. ("Pro Se"). Pro Se is a community-based, 501(c)(3) not-for-profit organization that provided hunger relief, nutrition, wellness, and human services to underserved populations throughout Cook County, IL from 2007 to 2012.

Throughout 2013, the organization was re-organized to provide necessary opportunities and resources to at-risk, troubled, or underserved adopted or foster children (0 – 17 years of age) and youth (18 – 21 years of age), and their families throughout the United States.

Programs

INKredible Kids Klub
This program was created by Iliyah and Imani, the Founders' daughters, to help the targeted population celebrate special occasions (birthdays, adoption, graduation, holidays, etc.) in their lives.

The Bootstrapers Band
This program partners the targeted population with professional mentors. Our mentors provide academic and vocational resources and social development and life skills training to our clients to help them chart their path towards recovery, resiliency, and becoming persons of excellence.

Healthy Bonds
This program promotes building healthy families by providing nutritional and wellness resources, caregiver's assistance, and diversity awareness training to adopted and foster families.

www.DinaeKnox.com